FOR DUST THOU ART

Crab Orchard Series in Poetry

Editor's Selection

T0164602

FOR DUST THOU ART

Timothy Liu

Crab Orchard Review

&

Southern Illinois University Press

CARBONDALE

Printed in the United States of America

08   07   06   05   4   3   2   1

The Crab Orchard Series in Poetry is a joint publishing venture of
Southern Illinois University Press and *Crab Orchard Review*. This series has
been made possible by the generous support of the Office of the President of
Southern Illinois University and the Office of the Vice Chancellor for Academic
Affairs and Provost at Southern Illinois University Carbondale.

Crab Orchard Series in Poetry Editor: Jon Tribble

Library of Congress Cataloging-in-Publication Data

Liu, Timothy.
   For dust thou art / Timothy Liu.
      p. cm. – (Crab Orchard series in poetry)
I. Title. II. Series: Crab Orchard award series in poetry.
PS3562.I799F67 2005
811'.54–dc22

0-8093-2652-3 (pbk. : alk. paper)   2005002182

Printed on recycled paper. ♻

The paper used in this publication meets the minimum requirements of
American National Standard for Information Sciences–Permanence of Paper for
Printed Library Materials, ANSI Z39.48-1992. ⊖

Contents

Acknowledgments

Thanks to the editors of the following publications, in which poems in this collection previously appeared:

Another Chicago Magazine—"Homo ex Humo"
Bloomsbury Review—"Revival"
The Canary—"What Remains"
Columbia: A Journal of Literature and Art—"Riding the Bull"
Crab Orchard Review—"Contemplating Disaster with the TV Off" and "Holy Law"
Crowd—parts 2 and 3 of "Fault Line"
Denver Quarterly—"At the Grand Bazaar" and "Besieged by Roses Shot from Quivers"
Dragonfire—"Dining Out after the Attack"
Drunken Boat—part 3 of "The Wealth of Nations"
Free Verse—"Malignant" and "Manifest Destiny"
Gargoyle—"Trespass"
Good Foot—"Ars Poetica"
Green Mountain Review—"Kamikaze Pilots in Paradise"
Gulf Coast—"On Hearing the Seven Last Words of Christ"
Hayden's Ferry Review—"Low Tide"
Kenyon Review—"Of Thee I Sing" and "On Broadway"
LIT—parts 1 and 3 of "The Wealth of Nations"
Michigan Quarterly Review—"A Prayer"
Mipoesias—"Beauty," "Terrorism," and "Vita Breva"
New Hampshire Review—"The Model"
Paris Review—"Pedophilic Ode" and "Rosetta Stone"
Pierian Springs—"Civilization and Its Discontents"
POM2—part 2 of "The Wealth of Nations"
The Quarterly—"Cemetery"
Quarterly West—"Self-Portrait as Seventies Teen"
Ribot—"Called Back" and "Ekphrasis in Excelsis Deo"
Salmagundi—"A Raid for the Bridal" and "A Valentine"
Seneca Review—"Anniversary"
Skanky Possum—"Disgrace," "Mayakovsky's Scream," "Orpheus at the Threshold," "Self-Portrait as Fucked-Up Mess," and "Something Coming"

Sonora Review—"Secret Combinations"
Verse—part 1 of "Fault Line" and "Tributaries"
VOLT—"Holding Pattern" and "Overcast"
Water-Stone—"For the New Year"
Web Conjunctions—"Dau Al Set"

"The Day After" was translated into Turkish by Önder Otçu and published in *Edebiyat Ve Elestiri* (Ankara).

"Homo ex Humo" was reprinted in *Wild and Whirling Words: A Poetic Conversation,* edited by H. L. Hix (Etruscan Press, 2003).

"For the New Year" was reprinted in *Old Glory: American War Poems from the Revolutionary War to the War on Terrorism,* edited by Robert Hedin (Persea, 2004).

For companions along the path for the past forty years: DA77 BT78 TC79 LB80 RK83 DL83 PP83 DB84 DM84 LL87 RL87 PW87 WG89 SJ89 BB90 CD90 LG90 AQ90 KC91 DH91 TB92 WB92 MW93 AZ93 JM96 EF98 KL98 DS98 NC01 PC01 MT01 BH02 CH02 JZ02 BB03 SM03 SS03 WM04, TM04, AH05.

ONE

"Perhaps the Light will prove another tyranny."

C. P. CAVAFY

Tributaries

Massive flows near falls where turbines run.

Hate or truce it flowers from within.

As habitat to penetrate a faggot's slender hips.

Flesh on flesh no matter who insists.

Pop-can scavengers skirting up our streets.

To survive another forty years the odds.

For sport down alleys lined with dirt a hole.

Nor understood just you weather it.

Baseball bats mere dust motes under eye.

In limited supply the scriptures that promote.

Revival

Two thousand cattle die across the state—
chickens watered down by hoses, barn fans
on the fritz. No worse off in the end
to succumb to the weather's slaughter—
steers competing with converts falling out

in Kansas City. So we fan ourselves
with hymnals, trying not to sing along
as splay-legged carcasses on the prairie
burst—stinking fly-blown ticking bombs
on feedlots gripped by a six-day wave.

Low Tide

The boiler room down below. Eyes of dockhands

fixed on a sculpted groin posing. How sailors buck

and rear to towel snaps as herds stampede into this

naval parade where showerheads hiss—the scent

of a stranger's ass randy under jockstraps slung

on bony hips burnished inside the sauna's rising

heat. Like cod medallions stewed in a saffron sauce—

linen falling off our laps as boytoys bathe. A taste

of oil and salt glistening on those toasted bodies

moon-pulled through the waves where buoys gently

bob—good head easier to get than a vintage Merlot

or a plate of mussels steaming in their own juice.

Ars Poetica

Indulge his more than ample mouth
where angle is all—his gnarled root
exposed where hornets dive-bomb
a beehive-do. Dear God—please
forgive those subway rats retreating
into a subterranean lair, only to be
found in the densely-layered nimbus
of some recurring dream—luminous
debris from a life so badly spent.

Homo ex Humo

A dawn washed clean by sun inviting stain

Bedroom windows that shudder each time

A train rides past a wrist a plaster cast

So pendulous on winter roads that wind

Through woods unmasked by spring a page

Torn from a book of birds love sometimes

Flies shells washed up on a mountainside

Where copies of testaceous malacology

Vanish into biblical illustration color

Patterns that conceal or reveal taxonomy

As sooty prints scumble across offshore

Refineries discarded bones to avoid an eye

That follows finger holes labile puzzles

Probe a cranial angle where catechisms

Come apart at the seams for dust thou

Art and to dust thou burnt-hair smell

Of a spider's legs dangling over halogen

Malignant

Dirt caked on a shovel
where a garden had been.

Some iris bulbs buried
under a blanket of pine.

That curtain of cloud
suddenly drawn aside —

then closing back again.

Trespass

The lake's ice breaking up in springtime's
sudden thaw, a father's drunken breath

pinning a child's shoulders to the bed—

mastodon bones ossifying below the floor
of that virgin bog. Must loss be sullied

by our need to love whatever survives?

Why give voice to any of that? Leave
those pages closed—case-studied tomes

a child could drown in. Such reticence

becomes us, dignity but a portable ark
that we shoulder through the wilderness.

Orpheus at the Threshold

The way she putzed around then dropped her panties to the floor.

The hourglass in her bedroom dependable as she.

In series was how the men arrived.

The openings of the body entered in a series not to be repeated.

A bathtub filled with roses browning at the edges.

A bloody sheet hung outside her hotel suite the only flag to be seen.

Descriptions of the act more memorable than the act itself.

What had been done on earth as it was in hell.

The whole house petal-strewn.

And the weight of lava stone healing bloodshot eyes.

Nerve-rope armored in its case of bone awaiting another's touch.

Self-Portrait as Fucked-Up Mess

A childhood kept
just out of reach

a knob high up
the pediatrician's

door with voices
on the other side

you never could
quite make out

going over charts
your tendency

to wake at night
and feast on turds

the rodents left
behind your bed.

Self-Portrait as Seventies Teen

      Muscles pulsing hard against that piece
of hair pie spread out on a Sunday insert
        flaunting Nautilus-homo-gang-raped
           joy wallowing in rugby mud, manly tools
        taking me back to a suburban
disco hell that summer I finally came
        jacking off to Blondie's "Heart of Glass"—
           jism plastered to a picture disc, no song
        quite able to turn *me* into a piece
of All-American ass—bestial ball-sack
        swinging as I got down on all fours
           to search for something lost in the shag—

Riding the Bull

Ready now to saddle up and ride out of those fiefdoms

you did not choose—unmet need assuming an attitude
of prayer. The romance going nowhere fast. Birdsong

caught in a net of cell-phone panic as the stock portfolio

dives. Prozaced to the nines and miles short of the next
free flight hi-jacked by an adult child who spurns those

kisses pulsing hot through a windshield kissed by stars.

ladies dying to help the homeless get in shape
during daily bible study sexual cycle
to rebuild self-confidence far beyond that figure
others crave a destitute white habit called
upon to drive two grams of alcohol all the way
to crash as press outside Le Petit Rameau
where speeding paparazzi race down glossy spreads
to be superfit a treadmill struggle doctors call
an ideal body-weight disorder a jar of exploding
peaches singling out a bottom-feeding flack
cashing-in on a sitcom stashed inside
a princess floating down that Venetian canal
where hunks caught flaunting cock for cash
cavort outside a hotel fire where rooftop rescuers
lower the rope on floozies whose Latin
makes us lurch a limited edition collector plate
ringed in 24 karat gold but an heirloom fit to serve
reduced-fat cheese while a doll mulls over
going under the knife distracted by nay-sayers
who launch a streamlined road to riches
speed-obsessed by limo love hell-bent-for-leather
backseat joyride requiring liquid asset
rent-free royal residence a flag-draped corpse
the cortege's centerpiece the biggest selling single
even surpassing Bing's "White Christmas"
a multi-million-dollar candle in the wind riding on
her flower-bedecked hearse all of us wanting
to touch her gold her Paris in the purse
like a La Gioconda devoured in the Louvre
by auto-focus flash frame by frame a hand-held
lens now zooming-in on Assisi monks
pinned down by chunks of Giotto in the latest quake
"La donna è mobile" wafting on through—

muffled-sob miscarriage reclining back
on sheepskin love gone wrong in a broken-off
key a stand-up monotone drone amplified
through brownout surge overheating rubber plants
that droop in the drowned man's house
with bathtub tributes to Marat scaling up
the unlaureled trellis of his crown his unspent
flower more useless now than sun-bleached spines
warping shelves of pine left nude by hands
more kin than kind refusing touch still tethered
to some all-seeing eye that finally came
unmoored in broken waves rocking on
in bourboned ice with orphans lost at sea
paddling under a mesh of cabled-steel supports
as can-can girls practiced thigh-high kicks
loosening up the dust from an antique chandelier
the evening cradled by derelict hips by hopes
disguised as a film-noir kiss that buds
anew in a slow-mo still each time our boy
disrobes more man than boy and more
than twice his age which leaves us breathless
darting in an out of spotlit corridors in search of
some affectionate sign a clue or a careless
labyrinthine glance sundering the line drawn firm
in backyard dirt crossed after all those years
haughty looks bullied us with plow and plunder
wide the secret cache filled with viral load
tunneling through the skull the pool at Holiday Inn
where a ghost-white piece of ass continued
doing laps and boys if boys were girls were blown
by each and every Andy or Abe joining hands
in a land of strung-out queens where storm-tossed
petals vulture-circled an ever-widening grave—

tired of all the gawking this conspicuous
consumption copycatting subcutaneous rumors
in a new frontier Melpomene mouse-clicks
through her high-speed phone line as journalists
sit enthralled on a pile of laptops discarded
in an over-caffeinated age bludgeoned
by homicidal TV rage in that morass of surly
stalemates contravening fiber found on a child's
labia where electrodes of a stun gun offered
solid proof some folding chairs afloat in that pool
overviewed by a sunroom facing west
her exercycle Schwinn already passing up
the twenty-eight-thousand-mile mark
as palpable cause a no-holds doubt cueing up
nostalgic stills uniforms encrusted with mud
and blood the frogging ripped an old piano
playing an adagio as cuirasses pile up in hecatombs
hallowed out by venerable pedigrees martinis
Gucci wherever peasants scavenge corpses
thrown into communal burial pits without heroic
diapasons of grandiosity sauntering through
this carnival where glory days are prelude
to gunshots on the Hill as interns got dolled-up
as rats continued gnawing through that well-
upholstered couch consigned to the Lincoln Room
where blasts of ultrasound tried keeping pests
at bay no poison no mess inside a corporate
payout at the center of our sand mandala
with Tibetan monks stalking around onstage
in silk sarongs as if America were still
a fucking dream Baryshnikov's bulge
fragrant as a girl from the Volga where factories
keep putting out after the Khrushchev thaw —

At the Grand Bazaar

Nodding the head once forward and down indicates a yes.

Nodding the head and eyebrows back signifies a no.

May also make the sound of "tsk."

Say *var*, "we have it"—more literally "it exists."

Certain signs can cause confusion.

Don't hold your hands apart at the desired length.

Chop your arm with the other hand perhaps about the elbow.

That is if you want a fish "this big."

That is if size matters at all.

May invite you to follow them by waving one of their hands.

Downward toward themselves in a scooping motion.

May even flutter their fingers.

But an upright finger would never occur.

Unless it were perceived as a vaguely obscene gesture.

Civilization and Its Discontents

Talking dirty but really a prig torn between
the shuck-and-jive of a great American

boom. His equipment more than adequate

for the job—all the chit chat of the city's idle
literati but mule dung cooked with beetles

forced down a child's throat. Vanity fueled

by cash and haute couture as bar maidens
dole out free harangues—vile remarks

unable to annihilate a father's sure contempt:

Cry me the same river twice whispered
in a dream not worth reporting to my shrink.

Secret Combinations

William Morgan given five hundred dollars and a horse.

Last seen crossing the Canadian border
while a shindig was being thrown at the Batavian Masonic Lodge—

More probably tied to a weighted cable.

Sent down Niagara Falls.

Swore by their heads that who should divulge whatsoever thing
shall lose their heads.

Binding myself to no less penalty than to have my skull struck off.

Of signs and secret combinations.

Mahhah-bone whispered on the five points of fellowship.

"Our throats to be cut from ear to ear and our tongues torn out
by their roots."

CAUTION   Shibboleth   Tubal Cain

Who leadeth them by the neck with a flaxen cord, a lambskin
girded about their loins.

Morgan   Monroe   Mormon

For truly I am Mahan, the master of this great secret.

Had caught her husband and Fanny Alger in loco extremis
with upraised arms square to the elbows.

Having brought upon themselves the full weight of displeasure.

Having trampled underfoot the customs of the past.

Lucinda Morgan left a widow in the bloom of her maidenhood.

A Valentine

Rose up to her power at a ripe Egyptian age.

Pushed up against the pyramid of time
as night abstained from telegraphy and steam—

"Some women younger at 70 than most at 17."

Impossible to document love's absurd excess
cradled in the paws of a desert Sphinx.

"Render unto Cæsar that which is Cæsar's."

Bus exhaust lacing a madonna's plaster sleeves—
the wings of a wayward luna moth

pinned against that speeding radiator grill.

Called Back

Between the blood clot and the bleeding out a long-distance line.

The dream's slow onset as the astral thread grew thin.

A hawk-headed god with a Wedjat-eye flanking either side.

The body but an altar with a lotus blossom on it.

"He takes the ship of a thousand cubits from end to end . . ."

Outspread wings of a mummified form seated on Sesostris' boat.

Rosetta Stone

No one to give voice to stone flakes swarmed with decadent
Coptic scripts still read in Arabic primers nor attempt
to understand extremities and implements as human shapes
took form according to the hermetic tracts of Diodorus Siculus
embodied in a single alphabetic word discovered after some
delay—black basalt slab a British heist coterminous
with the Nile's Bolbitine branch—French soldiers ordered
to demolish the foundations of a fort a demolition squad
ordered to ascertain the nature of that text lodged inside
an Institut Napoléon founded there unknown enchorial scripts
inked by skilled lithographers with India rubber rollers
till "a good impression had been made" had they remained
in the capital covered with cloth transferred to a warehouse
only to be exhibited to a public hungry for Ptolemaic stelae
with a winged disc sculpted-in—Horus' pendant uraeus
sporting crowns of an Upper and Lower Egypt reunited
by rings and ceremonial fans incised into stone—further
versions found on the walls of Isis' temple on the island
of Philae demotic equivalents identified by an orientalist

ARSINO   ALEXANDER   ALEXANDRIA

who labored under an "undulatory theory of light" until
work in damaged funerary papyrus led to a method of "and"

KING   PTOLEMY   EGYPT

neither literal nor nearly all incorrect at Karnak the cartouche
of a queen had known the obelisk's conclusion impossible
to tell what had been drawn up first "on the square surface"
"on the upper-side of the Atef crown" priestly privileges
listed in detail LIVING FOREVER   BELOVED OF PTAH
for all who entered the inner shrine for the robbing of the gods
for corn for taxes on byssus cloth neglected in former times
restored to its proper condition having gone to Lycopolis
by land or by sea in the Busirite nome fortified against a siege.

TWO

"My soul cleaveth unto the dust."

PSALMS 119:25

The Day After

looks overcast where rubble is being

removed—concrete, steel and bone
pulverized into ash, lovers disconnected

not twenty-four hours ago: turn on

the TV, two planes, etc. An ultralight?
A twin-engine prop having flown back out

the gaping holes? What the TV couldn't

show: hung-over day-traders late for work
stranded on our pier—cell-phone panic

on a ferry that was going nowhere

when the first plane struck, the second
on its way to a skyline fast reduced

to a pair of colossal torches whose fuel

was fuselage, our neighbors refusing
to watch the Towers collapse again

and again on those not to be reached until

every last Window on the World blew out,
Tower One's antenna knocking out

voices for miles around where children

had stood in the shadows of the Towers
just the day before, brand-new

back-to-school shoes in a Century 21 bag,

the neon sign at Krispy Kreme flashing
as they tasted their first hot glazed,

scattering crumbs for pigeons outside

Borders Bookstore. Before Borders itself
collapsed—"HOT NOW" no longer lit—

Century 21 closed until further notice.

A Prayer

A fast-busy signal.

A prerecorded message saying all circuits are busy will you please try
again.

And you do.

Again and again and again and again and again.

Eventually you will get through.

Eventually someone's going to find you.

Dig you out.

Your batteries are running low.

You must conserve your energy.

You think you know where you are.

At least where you were when it all came crashing down.

What you are is an abstract entity.

A victim.

Almost a casualty.

Given time.

You wonder how many others.

We wonder how many others.

We must do something.

Below 14th the streets are closed.

Without i.d. we would surely get arrested.

An operation already underway.

Another building about to collapse.

Another building that has just collapsed.

Are you still breathing?

Is the line still busy?

Are you able to get through?

Are you still trying to get through?

And what could you possibly say that hasn't been said already?

Where dogs are sniffing through the rubble.

Where another sun is setting.

Where batteries are going dead.

Where batteries have gone dead.

On Broadway

The planes in the sky still half-empty as ticket sales

plummet. At curtain call, Hedda Gabler dusted off
the gunpowder from her petticoats before thanking us

for coming, a show still in previews, uncertain if

the house would be empty or full come opening night,
the Emmys postponed though Access Hollywood's

back on the air. The St. Petersburg Chamber Orchestra

trying to rebook, eager to risk their lives in order to
perform Rachmaninov's "Vespers." So much rehearsal

wasted. So many bodies to recover. What was to be

must settle for what is—the Towers renamed "the Pile"—
Hedda Gabler better off dead than allowed to play

in boredom—a sure-fire ending staged night after night.

Dining Out after the Attack

A dinner party for eight. The check arrived
accompanied by shock and disbelief for such
a mediocre meal: two hundred fifty dollars
per person. Are you sure there hasn't been
some kind of huge mistake? "We take VISA,
American Express also." But who ordered
the nine-hundred-dollar bottle of champagne?
The Afghan over there. Make him pay for it.

Holy Law

Someone gets five years for plowing his
car into a mosque. Perhaps he was on

a suicide mission. Some call it a history
written in sand and blood as the campaign

shifts. Children foraging dust. Dead vines
sold for wood on the outskirts of Kabul —

the Shamili plain laid waste. Never mind
Don't Ask, Don't Tell or the whereabouts

of Osama diverting our nation's attention
from a top-to-bottom review of ocean

policy needed to keep the swordfish steaks
coming to our tables—polluted runoff

largely to blame for the fishless dead zone
of the Gulf wherever border-crossing

Chicanos quote Aztec law requiring all
homosexuals to be disemboweled at once—

Ready-Mades

Missing-persons photos plastered onto a van.

Pockets of air beneath the rubble.

Welcome then to the world community.

Candle-lit vigils held by volunteers.

As survivors circle the Armory for any news.

This the place where Duchamp showed?

Morgan Stanley, Merrill Lynch.

South of Pittsburgh shot down by the Feds.

Let's smoke 'em out of their holes!

Imagine a president saying that.

Offshore where a Wildlife Preserve had been.

Terrorism

Neither fiction nor a discourse
but flowers. The liminal edge
of what has been—the suspension
of daily activity where what is
possible outweighs the probable
crisis ever bridging backwards
into history. Prophecies to explain
why eyes are glued to glass,
why laughter seems unable
to return to the streets just yet
though "it's safer now to travel
than ever," messages of love
scrawled by children onto strips
of construction paper pasted
onto an American flag delivered
to a firehouse where passers-by
stop to weep. *Honey, is that
a dumpster or the smell of . . . ?*
passed on in whispers—the upper
level deck of the sight-seeing bus
filling up again. Should what was
be rebuilt? Should ashes be smeared
across our foreheads, our clothing
rent instead of lighting candles
and leaving bouquets under
the photos of those still missing?
More and more forced to take
public transportation—the carpool
rule requiring us to "buddy-up"
as we play that game of holding
our breaths as long as we can
riding through the Lincoln Tunnel—
me on my cell telling you this,
wasting away my anytime minutes
while the word "crusade" is banished
from our President's lexicon—

reported incidents of road rage
down, your flag pin but a show
of solidarity if not a talisman
warding off those baseball bats
one Arab said to another seated
next to me—none of it really
any good against anthrax, plague
or vx gas, not even surgical
masks carried in our packs for luck.

Of Thee I Sing

The claim of a hoax more than a hoax underneath our skirts

where oceanic musings froth at the mouth—patrons fed up
with the Feds still kowtowing to that souped-up pimpmobile

piling on the schmooze. The Beltway really cooking now

with stockpiled nukes from Russia missing—ten kilograms
enough to pack a suitcase bomb and liquefy storefront glass—

a stolen ramp badge last seen slung on some hijacker's neck.

Contemplating Disaster with the TV Off

Should we turn the news back on? Most bridges and tunnels
have reopened. Once again we can hear the sound of a jet
passing overhead. We even went out for a gallon of water

at a deli downstairs called US1. Our Middle-Eastern clerk
has taken to wearing a golden cross, American flags plastered
on a business that seems to be doing okay as we give a nod

and race back up five flights of stairs where the TV remains
off. The cell phone's ringing now (how else get through?)
and it's Jimmy who informs us that his father's part-Lebanese,

Jimmy who passes for white, whose paranoid-schizophrenic
father assures him not to worry about everything going on—
a dad with some vets gathered round a TV in the mental ward.

Sitting Still

It takes
awhile

to be able

to do
just that.

An Inferno

Makeshift tents dotting the site
where demo experts demolish

the demolished. Mangled I-beams

graffitied with their last known
address in some attempt to map

the collapse. Plans to rebuild

abuzz where all goes on ahead
of schedule—spray-painted codes

marking bodies that were heard,

not reached. A fireman's boot
exhumed at last—strange trophy

from rubble still too hot to touch.

Vita Breva

To eke out spiritus on a bomb-damaged site.

The task of earning one's daily bread.

"No matter on what grounds."

Full of leisure and pleasureful abandon.

Inventing rules to keep the spoils.

Removed from war the task.

Having made my body come again again.

Makeshift morgues sprouting up all over town.

To get ourselves "disappeared."

However the plea.

Dusted about with sentiments to soften the blow.

Tenderness in a Dark Age

A case of ass. Just what did we think
we were doing washing ourselves up

with soap? Who said it was a privilege

to have hitchhiked on an interstate
where prison crews had been? "Each

new pair of shoes, a different walk,"

the warden said, some of us juiced
on Modafinil for the all-night watch—

October's "total goat fuck" classified

haberdash. Just remember: if love
goes south, it's all bread and butter

in the end and not a you among those

seated in the opera house that sinks
a quarter inch each year—Chinook

helicopters disgorging staging areas

in a covert "snoop and poop"—all of it
said without a single crease across

your brow as bounty hunters looked

the other way. Wanting to make it
to your birthday had a different feel

than wanting to simply live a long life.

For the New Year

What was America ever about
if not "Full Frontal Fashion"
if not McDonald's, Wendy's, and dropping rations
from a plane onto a war-torn landscape—
reports of Bin Laden smuggled out
in a head to floor-length burkah
across poppy fields fertilized with roadside corpses
overjacked on smack
on search & seizure / sneak & peak / whatever it takes
a hundred-thousand hits alone this week
on bushorchimp.com
lest we forget the sweet ache in our groins
after so much friction trying
to fuck in every room of the house
while B-52s carpet-bombed
Kabul, Kandahar and Mazar-i-Sharif
till Afghanistan in its disgrace
like the faceless face of a Bamian Buddha
offered up its landmined limbs and amputated feet
to the God of Holy Law
underpants dangling on the chandelier
our wasted jizz enough to repopulate an entire nation
eager to fly those Friendly Skies again—
racial profiling ratcheted up
at security checks flanked by M-16s
and minimum wage
as anthraxed legions bulldozed through the lungs
of a child just getting born—

Beauty

Hundreds of bodies identified. Others
found only in parts. A demand
        for Nostradamus on the rise: *In the city*
            of York, there will be a great collapse—
        two twin brothers torn apart by a third
big war to begin when the city burns—
        tents from Fashion Week in Bryant Park sponsored
            by Mercedes Benz now converted
        into staging areas for the dead—too late
for the Emmys though Miss America
        will go on as the seventy-two virgins
            of Paradise welcome the martyrs in—

Elegy for Oum Kolsoum Written Across the Sky

The century's greatest Arabic voice
as cause for swoon as mourners by the millions
lined the Cairo streets to catch a glimpse
of her corpse. Gone is that most rare of wines
that spilled into a desert where caged cocks
perched on sills served as an early
warning system for chemical attacks—
aggressive tactics that delivered designer
opiates to those of us lining up
to trade our hash pipes in—pleasure reduced
to "Ala Balad El Mahboub" muzaked
through the roof. Didn't you know while women
only want to be adored, men only
want to get laid?—the gender wars hard-wired
on both sides of the globe—to don or not
to don a scarf the only question
on the minds of Muslim women who chain
themselves to those university gates
in Istanbul, never mind Iran, never mind
the Persian Gulf basking like a swimming pool
cast in the shape of a casting couch
any F-16 can see before it gets shot down—

Kamikaze Pilots in Paradise

Marriage a series of monologues where discussions were eschewed.

All history but a reconstruction of an undetectable past.

With passages marked in red recited in unison.

Circumscribed like the villages of endogamous Mormondom.

Outcast or apologist we were forced to play.

To rehearse a ritual wherein no syllable could be changed.

To maintain our place by reinscribing fame.

This then was how we chose to live with vows we learned by rote.

A love most amateur chronicled verbatim.

Standing creedless we longed for forms of spiritual exercise.

Sodomy and depravity all humans are heir to.

As corpses of the diseased were catapulted over walls.

Every possible pleasure to be indulged for the world was at an end.

THREE

"It is better to be crushed jade than a brick."

CHINESE PROVERB

The Book of Abraham

I am the Provider

Most exalted and very glorious

A virile bull without equal

That Mighty God

In the Sun Temple in Heliopolis

O God of the Sleeping Ones

From the time of the Creation

O Mighty God

Lord of heaven and earth

Of the hereafter

And of His great waters

May the soul of Osiris Shishaq

Be granted life

May this tomb never be

Desecrated

And may this soul and its Lord

Never be desecrated

In the hereafter

The Model

Our decrepit tree house
    was only an approximation
        for what the world was like—

a childhood assembled
    with whatever was on hand—
        a constellation of nail heads

that held it all together.

Anniversary

To speak no ill. To resist locutions

torqued from one hard-scrabble night
to the next recurrent myth—primordial

forms fueled by drink and the day's

minutiae a tarantella of operatic forms
flung into the congested turbulence

of a *prix-fixe* dream, the latent vows

which gave themselves away to marital
sleights-of-hand as we felt we could

afford the caffeine of successive cups

starting to kick in now at the opening
bars of an unscored aria, my voice

that icy pitcher waiting to be poured—

On Hearing the Seven Last Words of Christ

Today there was sun, tomorrow
snow, and the day after? To see
your face, the sound of your voice
that would make more splendid
this room where I sleep filled
with one of Haydn's late quartets
in a key I cannot name because
everything keeps on shifting
from where it began and I've lost
my frame of reference, the pitches
altered by the room's acoustics
and by mood, splendid, this state
of mind immersed in so much
being the inhuman has begun to
flower in its cosmic machinations
cold and green in their distant
radiance immune to feeling
what can be known were it not
for the absence that now attends it.

Dau Al Set

Vocalise haunted still by faces smeared with ash.

Depressed all winter long he thwarts his captive breath.

If only we could plunder rumors kept well guarded.

But are you there and are we troubling you?

The stars suffused with aspects no one can discern.

A maiden warming up to a widow who shields her face.

Who's to say our *ch'i* might not suddenly bloom.

Or rival a sage's flowering arms await the call.

The ceiling clay shouldered-in by solemn monks.

An oracle to be chosen where the bottle stood uncorked.

Lips without song useless as the hours pass.

Who asks for bread instead of stone flying overhead?

A sickness in the blood crowned with fire.

Renounce the troth or spare us six-winged seraphim.

Too much perhaps desired glazed with pearly glow.

As he forsook the root to try the bones again.

In mansions we cannot enter wider than this world.

Mayakovsky's Scream

Caught in the spotlight's glare—
poets getting drunk on their own

blood. How secret indiscretions

soiled the family nest—childhood
melting on a fornicator's tongue

while a magnifying glass burned

holes into the Magnum Opus—
nostalgia's shade a load of leaves

from a tree that no longer stands.

Manifest Destiny

Clouds of razor wire hovering over brick.

Mammograms on boxes lit from within.

With winter in one world and spring next door.

Begin again where clients mill about.

Old scars cradled in their own geography.

Even a mother's care cannot annul.

Nor the shape of that runaway shopping cart.

What Remains

A Dalí etching pinned beneath a mat
hardly acid-free. Like pages torn
from an atlas mapping out another time.
A storm front coming on. What then
shall we make of star-script etched
into the corners of the mind—clusters
of mahogany grapes carved into
that headboard left in a cold boudoir
long after the bridal train has gone—

Overcast

He says he feels more and more like the wife, meaning more
like furniture. An arrangement left on the coffee table to keep

appearances up. Perhaps we all can feel the silence she feels
smothered by—laughter's good weather suffused with bloom,

the streets but part of a siren song lovers walk without alarm.
Like gold that's sunk to the ocean floor—childhood's heavy

gold sinking even now as voices huddle outside the bedroom
door—our children as yet unkissed by dawn's advancing call.

Pedophilic Ode

"Ran afoul my nature to spend some time
in prison. To think
                    on what I'd done:
does a butcher not know each of his pigs
nor the gentle curve of wood
                              cleaved
by steady pounding? Why else this need
to have a child play mirror
                        to what I am?
Group therapy no match for the gods
buried in each body
                    sauntering past.
Why this wanting to also become a god—
paradise be but ghost
                    to what they were."

Cemetery

The earth wounded

by stone. Nothing
heals. Not birds

singing nor insects

underground.
There is a hunger

beyond all feeding,

a mouth that will
suck the marrow

out of our bones—

Fault Line

ash pits on the beach where fires had been the galleys left unread the wind a second round

of chemo turning cheekbones into corpse impromptus left in situ to make our mark without

reward nor grant the time lukewarm as intentions are a bathtub holding flood nor waterfall

that kayak's vertical descent alone alone as road maps catching sail on pavement lined

with Kool-Aid stands and sacramental cyanide recalled in a mother's voice a sea of ice plant

offering up its islands of Monet where moonlit cows and mortgages root down into the bones

of us detritus scattered along this desolate coast fenced-in by hills the color of offshore fog dawn's arrows poised for flight near banquet tables that run the entire length of heaven

while radio signals from Alabama disrupt a late quartet haunted by squawks and jeers

that taunt us still all those frat boys wanting nothing but release their tattooed anchors

sinking beneath black light where disco reigns triumphant with death not far behind

our voices weak without the flesh without that white macaw and cockatoo chanting rote

affections asking us to pay attention where lights go down on love letters scrawled by

hand stacked shoulder-high to the wind as newlyweds now vanish behind a storm of rice

violations teething throaty laughs as juveniles take a blowtorch to that stray some sissies

hypnotized by a casual bulge reciting verses that Rumi wrote in praise of Shams buried

under mud that slid through windows nestled high on hills as footsteps of past masters fit

stifling masks onto pressed hams spied through shower glass in that parade of tongues

licking tender egos foisted onto thrones bejeweled with envy and regret where trolls get

off on jocks peeling off their shorts on a private beach fenced-in by porno stills unspooled

on the kitchen floor some hang-up calls the police can't trace as hurricanes come and go

Something Coming

Confessions heard by a chaplain aboard the cruise.

Having relegated the work of feeling.

Some wicked static on a 1-900 phone-sex line.

The problematics of a simulacral culture.

Bush still leading Gore by 344.

Who enjoys the sight of a freshly paddled ass?

Like two men of the same mind.

One grows more suspicious of lyric self-reflection.

Disgrace

Porcelain-throned Aphrodite—

don't leave me sitting here
on a public john with no one

to adore, not even a troll,

my cock-tip weeping tears
for thy annulment, heavenly

service charioting our fears

to a far-off realm security
won't intrude upon—torsos

bronzed by piss, smeared

with lordly shit so ages hence
might marvel how I chose

to defy such a world as this—

Besieged by Roses Shot from Quivers

With alchemists gathering dew off leafy shrubs at dawn.

A sprig of rue hung above the cattle-shed door.

Where dried mullein dipped in fat had been lit up as a torch.

Before the brothel-heavy afternoon settled in.

Under that vaulted dome some called the castle of love.

Untold chivalric escapades soon espied.

Seated ladies sewing chaplets flanked by a turf bench.

By plasters applied to the abdomen to aid in their conception.

Lavender tied in bundles for chastity's preserve.

Blackouts to outlast five hundred years.

Between the villa and the garden where scholars have failed.

A Raid for the Bridal

Such days of spent-bud panoply as the petaled horde
unfolds—waxy leaves caught gleaming in a sylvan

decadence. To seek what maidenhead abhors—

each of us wading through love's intolerable flood.
Chivalric angst where arrows strike the lowest mark.

How else get down to the essential self freed

from headache and applause, panhandled man-love
martyrdom there on the brink of death?—offstage

noises dashing us with amorous wet where drunken

pre-dawn infomercial drone betroths us to such
shipwreck foundering at the storm's climactic ebb.

Ekphrasis in Excelsis Deo

Dancers dead of AIDS rollicking through the pews.

Trying to rectify the sex-policed positions.

Classically trained in arrogance they're paid to do.

Entirely caught in a spiritual undertow.

The audience disengaged.

Nothing mythic about their looks so furtive as they flee.

Behind a choice predella's gold leaf left intact.

A martyr crowned with thorns.

Finished now with pop-up-books come what may.

Holding Pattern

visibility climbing as dawn kicks into higher gear our fingers clutching fix-it

manuals gilded tomes in a terminal stalls an inboard fan cowl deactivating edge

slats postal routes we must retract to subdue that shirtless slithering through

the park like wolves like doves who mate for life best sprig as affections some

times are more rare than kneecaps rocking in a tub red tip of cock peaking over

those postdiluvian waterlines you fraud you rain-torn address book left lilting

in late october sun undone to the nines your swollen cathedral bells as deacons

leer atop a mermaid's undulating tongue why else unwind tight rubber bands undo

nuptial vows we who are a biplane lost in snow guided through by a single flare

Other Books in the Crab Orchard Series in Poetry